11.44

DISASTER!
EARTHQUAKES

By Dennis Brindell Fradin

Consultant:
   Finley C. Bishop, Ph.D.
   Assistant Professor of Geological Sciences
   Northwestern University
   Evanston, Illinois

 CHILDRENS PRESS, CHICAGO

These homes in the Anchorage residential development of Turnagain Heights were destroyed in the landslide caused by the 1964 earthquake in Alaska.

For my wife, Judith

For their help, the author thanks:

*Thomas Burdette of the Office of Earthquake Studies in Menlo
    Park, California
Angelo Liberati of the Onditalia Broadcasting Company
Patricia Chiappetta of the Production Department, Childrens Press
Anna Andreotti of the Italian Cultural Center
Ralph De Parolis of the Italian Consulate*

Library of Congress Cataloging in Publication Data

Fradin, Dennis B.
  Earthquakes.

  (Disaster!)
  Summary: Discusses why the earth quakes,
how earthquakes kill and destroy, and how to
predict and prepare for earthquakes. Also
describes some famous earthquakes, including the
one that struck southern Italy in 1980.
  1. Earthquakes—Juvenile literature.
[1. Earthquakes. 2. Italy, Southern—Earthquake, 1980] I. Title. II. Series: Fradin,
Dennis B. Disaster!
QE521.3.F73   551.2'2   81-12263
ISBN 0-516-00853-6   AACR2

TABLE OF CONTENTS

*Above: A fireman walks through the rubble of the village of Santomena,
one of the hundred towns in southern Italy damaged or destroyed during
the earthquake of November 23, 1980.
Below: In the town of Laviano, a mother looks down at her sixteen-year-old
son, one of the thousands of victims of the earthquake in southern Italy.*

1/SOUTHERN ITALY-1980

There was no warning—at least none that was detected. At 7:36 P.M. on November 23, 1980, southern Italy was struck by a strong earthquake. The ground shook for about a minute. During that time, homes and apartments toppled as if they were toys. Churches, schools, and stores caved in. When the earth stopped shaking, much of southern Italy looked as if it had been hit by a huge bomb. Thousands of people were dead. Thousands more lay trapped beneath collapsed buildings.

"Eighty percent of Sant'Angelo dei Lombardi has been destroyed," one Italian official reported by radio. "Hundreds of people are buried under the rubble." Many other towns had suffered the same fate.

Throughout southern Italy, people dug relatives and friends out of the ruins. Some of the victims were pulled out alive. More were not. One man pulled away debris for twelve straight hours until he reached his trapped son. The boy died in his arms. The streets were filled with crying people who had lost their loved ones.

It is difficult to plan for a tragedy in which a hundred towns might be damaged or destroyed. But in this case, much suffering and death could have been prevented. The Italian government was very slow in organizing rescue units. Rescue efforts also were delayed by bad weather, wrecked roads, and fallen telephone lines. Another problem was the huge area involved—10,000 square miles.

It was several days before rescue workers reached many of the stricken areas. But some of those trapped beneath the ruins were still alive. Some could be heard calling for help.

Microphones were lowered into the ruins to detect heartbeats and breathing of those too badly hurt to call.

When they found signs of life, the rescue workers dug frantically. At a fallen hospital, three babies were rescued. Three days after the quake, a rescue dog began barking at a ruined house in Lioni. The dog had been trained to bark when it smelled a human being—alive or dead—beneath the rubble. Workers dug out a ten-year-old boy. "Everything fell down, didn't it?" the boy said when he was brought out into the daylight. "What a long night!"

In one small town, three elderly people were rescued from their cellar fifteen days after the quake. They had survived by drinking wine and eating hot peppers. These three may have been the last survivors pulled from a wrecked building. After fifteen days, it was no longer a rescue operation. It had become a matter of retrieving bodies.

Rescue workers carry an elderly woman from the wreckage of her home in Avellino.

The earthquake completely destroyed the mountain village of Castelnuovo Conzo.

For the survivors, there were great problems. More than 300,000 had lost their homes. People built campfires and slept in fields and streets. But it was too cold for them to remain outside all winter. Many took refuge in tents. Some moved into cars or pickup trucks. Trailers, campers, and even train cars were moved in to house people.

People from many countries helped the Italian government take clothes, blankets, and food to the survivors. But some did not receive help in time. Hunger, cold, and disease claimed the lives of many who might have lived—if the Italian government had been better prepared for an earthquake.

In the small mountain town of Balvano, earthquake survivors gathered in open squares for safety (above).

Months after the quake, people were still living in tents and train cars. They were still cooking their food over open fires. Their drinking water was brought to them in bottles or plastic containers. Mountains of bricks, fragments of furniture, and pieces of buildings lay piled up on city streets. Cars that had been crushed by falling walls lay at the curbsides. Some buildings that were still standing had cracked walls and looked ready to fall.

The death toll in this quake topped 3,000. As Italian earthquakes go, this one was major, but not the worst ever. The 1908 quake at Messina, Italy killed 85,000 persons. In the past century, more than twenty major quakes have struck Italy. Each time, the survivors have rebuilt their towns knowing that future earthquakes might destroy them once again.

2/SURVIVORS - ITALY, 1980

Scientists know what causes earthquakes. But only people who have survived one know what they feel like. Here are the stories of several survivors of the 1980 quake in Italy.

Nick Palermo

Four months after the earthquake—and 5,000 miles from home—Nick Palermo's eyes filled with tears as he told of digging bodies out of the rubble.

On November 23, 1980, twenty-three-year-old Palermo was riding in a bus. He was on his way from his hometown of Castelvetere Sul Calore to the city of Salerno, where he attended college. At 7:36 P.M., the bus suddenly began to shake and veer.

"At first we all thought it was a flat tire," Nick remembered. "Then we saw houses toppling all around us and people running and screaming. We realized it was an earthquake."

The bus was a good place to survive the quake. Its shock absorbers had been designed to withstand bumpy roads. They helped the bus remain upright on the wildly bucking ground.

"When I saw that the bus was safe, I began to worry about my family and friends in my hometown," continued Nick. He had good reason to worry. A radio news flash reported that the town next to Nick's had been totally destroyed.

The bus continued on to Salerno. Many buildings still standing in Salerno were unsafe. So Nick slept on the street with hundreds of others. Early the next morning, he

In the aftermath of the earthquake, Nick Palermo helped the people in the badly stricken towns of Lioni (above) and nearby Sant' Angelo dei Lombardi.

hitchhiked back to Castelvetere Sul Calore. He found that his family was safe. A few houses had fallen and the insides of some were damaged. But the town had not been hit as hard as many others.

Nick decided to help the people in some badly stricken towns. He hitchhiked to the town of Sant'Angelo dei Lombardi, where many people had been killed or injured. For the next three weeks, Nick searched for bodies in the rubble. He also helped put up tents for the living in Sant'Angelo and in nearby Lioni.

*This eight-year-old girl (left)
was one of the few persons
rescued from under the rubble
in Sant 'Angelo dei Lombardi.
Above: Women of Volturara Irpina
stop to pray before a statue
of the Madonna that somehow
remained intact during the
earthquake that rocked the village.*

"The only way to pull the bodies out was with our hands,
ropes, and shovels. Cement and rocks had buried everything.
There was a bar in Sant'Angelo where people had gathered to
watch a soccer game on TV. It was destroyed. About thirty
bodies were dug out of there.

"For about seven days there was no outside help at all. We
had to manage for ourselves. There were many injured. And
it was freezing out and people were getting sick. Hospitals
were set up in houses that were still standing. Doctors and
medical students volunteered to help."

Each night, Nick hitchhiked back to his hometown. No one
there wanted to sleep in a house that might collapse at any
time. So Nick and the other townspeople spent the nights in
tents, pickup trucks, and cars. They went into their homes
only to gather food, which they cooked outside over big fires.

Although Nick dug bodies from the rubble and set up tents
for twenty-one days, only once did he witness a rescue. "One
morning in Sant'Angelo I saw a fireman pulling out rock and
sand with his hands. He had been digging all night. He was
just pulling out a girl when I got there. She was all right."

In December, Nick Palermo's family moved into the home of a friend in Italy. Nick came to live temporarily with his uncle and aunt in the United States.

In the home of his aunt and uncle, Nick told of one set of images that will always haunt him. He will never forget the faces of the people when they saw the bodies of their loved ones pulled from the debris.

"Husbands saw that their wives were dead and parents saw their children. People were screaming for their families. Many still didn't believe that it actually had happened.

"Who could believe that such a thing could happen in just one minute?"

Vincenzo Trombetta

On the evening of November 23, 1980, Vincenzo Trombetta went into a bar in Serino, Italy. The eighty-two-year-old retired tailor planned to play some cards with friends. Then he would eat dinner at the bar. Trombetta still carried wounds from World War I. But his life was peaceful now. In the small town of Serino it should have remained peaceful.

"I was ordering something to eat when the earthquake hit," Trombetta recalled four months later. "Bottles went flying. Tables toppled. Everything was shaking. We couldn't even see to get out the door because the earthquake had knocked the lights out."

In those few seconds, many houses in Serino fell. But the ten people in the bar were lucky. The building withstood the quake. When the earth stopped shaking, Trombetta and the others made their way out the door.

"As I headed to my house I saw people running around and

screaming," said Trombetta. "Some had blood coming from their heads." When Trombetta reached his house, he saw that it looked fine from the front. But the entire back wall had fallen to the ground and part of the roof had caved in. On that first night, Trombetta joined some people in the town square. They built a big fire to keep warm.

The next day, Trombetta walked around Serino. "A river goes through the town. On one side of the river many of the buildings were down. The ones on the other side were cracked and damaged, but they were still standing.

"Several dozen people in our town died in the earthquake. One was a woman who had been a friend of mine. She and her son had tried to leave their house when the quake hit. She was just a little bit behind the son. He made it out, but then the house caved in and killed her.

"I also saw a two-story house that had caved in. The people on the first floor made it out in time. But a woman on the second floor had just picked up her baby to try to save it when the house fell. They were both dug out—dead."

Trombetta slept outside by the fire for two more days. But then people began to move into cars and tents. Small quakes, called *aftershocks,* struck southern Italy in the days after the big earthquake. Trombetta didn't know if his house would withstand the aftershocks. But at eighty-two, he didn't want to live in a tent or a car. He decided to move back into his house and take his chances.

Trombetta found a corner of the house where the walls looked pretty solid. "I dragged a cot into that corner. I slept there for twenty nights. I ate canned foods that I had in the house."

Italy's 1980-81 winter was very cold and rainy. Trombetta kept the fireplace going day and night to keep warm. But at

Vincenzo Trombetta

night, rainwater leaked through the roof and splashed on him. "I figured out a way to keep dry," he said. "I slept beneath an open umbrella."

Nevertheless, Trombetta developed a bad cold. He didn't want to go to the hospital that had been set up in a church building. Badly injured people needed those beds. So in late December, Vincenzo Trombetta decided to leave the town where he had lived for most of his eighty-two years. He came to the United States to live with a daughter.

Trombetta was in bad shape when he arrived in the United States. His family feared that he wouldn't live. It wasn't only the chest cold. He was in shock from the whole experience. He shook continually. He couldn't talk. But after spending several weeks with his family, he began to recover.

"I'll never go back to Italy," said Vincenzo Trombetta. "There's nothing for me there now. No home. Nothing. But the saddest part wasn't the buildings. The saddest part was the people who died."

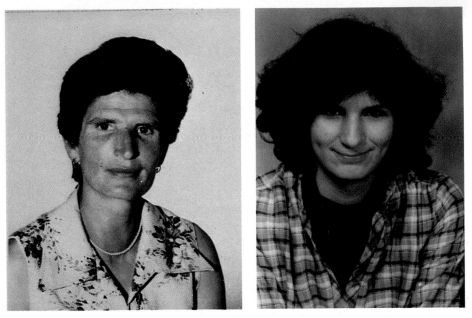

Geraldina Alfano (left) and her daughter Camilla

Geraldina Alfano

"The animals knew that something was wrong before the earthquake," Geraldina Alfano said four months later. "The cows, horses, chickens, and dogs were making very loud noises. The dogs, especially, seemed to know that something was wrong."

On the night of November 23, 1980, Geraldina Alfano listened to the animals' strange noises coming from outside. She was making dinner for her husband and their six children. The Alfanos lived on a farm outside the small town of Santo Stefano Del Sole. They often worried about their crops of potatoes and corn. But an earthquake was the furthest thing from their minds.

"I was in the kitchen when all of a sudden the lights went out and the floor started going up and down and throwing us all over the house. My husband knew right away that it was an earthquake. He said that we should take the children out of the house.

"We couldn't get out the door because it was already blocked by fallen things. Our only way out was through the window. Our whole house fell just after we climbed out."

Once outside, the Alfanos were safe. But they had a big worry. Two of their sons had been playing in the town when the quake struck. Geraldina and her husband, Gaetano, were just starting out to search for them when the boys came home screaming and crying.

When they saw that the boys were safe, Mr. and Mrs. Alfano began to worry about relatives and friends in town. Geraldina Alfano was thirty-seven years old and seven months pregnant. Nevertheless, she ran almost a mile into town. First she checked to see if her mother had survived the quake.

"My mother was all right, but in the town I found a friend who had been struck on the head by a falling rock. She lay there with blood coming out of her head. A car came by and we carried her to it. She was taken to a hospital, but she went into a coma and died a week later.

"Meanwhile, my husband had come across an old couple in town who were buried under their fallen house. My husband was trying to dig them out when a big brick fell and hit the woman on the side of her head. The husband was pulled out safely but the woman died."

The Alfanos stayed up most of the night helping their friends and neighbors in town. At about two in the morning, they returned to what was left of their house.

Their first problem was finding a place to sleep. They found some plastic that was used to cover their crops on cold nights. They used it to make four tents. Homeless friends and relatives came to the Alfano farm and joined them in the tents.

During the next several days, the Alfanos went into their wrecked house to pull out some clothes and blankets. They also retrieved some furniture that hadn't been destroyed.

"We lived in those homemade tents for fifteen days," said Mrs. Alfano. "Just to keep warm we slept almost on top of each other. We cooked our food on an open fire. But there was so much rain that the fire kept going out.

"We were luckier than many others, though. We had cows on our farm to give us milk, and I made cheese from the milk. After fifteen days, things got better because the government brought in trailers for us to live in."

By that time, however, their son Vito was sick with a cough and a fever. "I decided to take Vito to America. I especially wanted to go to America to have my baby. My husband stayed in Italy to rebuild our house."

In December of 1980, Geraldina Alfano, her son Vito, and two other children went to live temporarily with relatives in the United States. Two months after the earthquake, Geraldina Alfano gave birth to a baby boy.

Vito Alfano

When the quake hit, eleven-year-old Vito Alfano was playing outside the town's church with his brother and some friends.

"All of a sudden I saw houses falling and rocks flying," he remembered. "I saw the big church go to pieces. I didn't know it was an earthquake. I thought it was the end of the world.

"I was so scared all I could do was run home. My family was very glad to see my brother and me. One of my friends in

Vito Alfano

our town died, though, when a building fell on top of him. The priest in the church died, too.''

In the days after the quake, Vito's parents needed some potatoes and corn that were stored in the cellar of their house. They asked Vito to go down into the cellar to get the food. ''But I just couldn't go down there,'' he remembered. ''I kept thinking another earthquake would come and bury me inside the house.''

After the quake, Vito got sick. He had a fever and a bad cough. A doctor from the town came and gave him some medicine. But he didn't fully recover until shortly before he left Italy.

The day after Christmas, 1980, Vito arrived with his mother in the United States. ''It felt really good to be able to sleep inside a house in a bed,'' Vito said. ''It was a lot warmer than the tent.

''I still think about the earthquake. When I hear a truck or a loud car or a fire engine go by, it reminds me of the night when everything fell.''

3/WHY THE EARTH QUAKES

Ancient people did not understand the causes of earthquakes. So they made up stories to explain them.

The ancient Greeks said that the god Atlas balanced the world on his shoulders. The world was very heavy, so Atlas shifted the weight from shoulder to shoulder. When he did that, the earth shook.

The people of India decided that the world was balanced on the head of an elephant that sat on the back of a tortoise. Whenever one of the animals moved a bit, the result was an earthquake.

Old Russian stories tell of a giant god who rode across the ice fields on a dogsled. The dogs had fleas. When they scratched the fleas, the earth trembled.

The Algonkian Indians of North America said that the world rode on the back of the Great Tortoise. Some Japanese people thought that it was carried about by a giant catfish. In

South America, people said that the world sat on the back of a whale. In all these stories, earthquakes were said to occur when the animals moved about.

Christian and Jewish people of long ago thought that earthquakes were sent by God to punish people. The eighteenth Psalm in the Old Testament states that when God was angry ". . . the earth shook and trembled; the foundations also of the hills moved and were shaken. . . ." In the New Testament, St. Matthew describes an earthquake that took place on the day that Jesus was crucified: ". . . and the earth did quake, and the rocks rent. . . ."

Not until 1760 did English scientist John Mitchell conclude that earthquakes have something to do with massive movements of rocks. But even the few who believed this thought that these movements were caused by underground explosions. In 1859, earthquake science was advanced when Irish engineer Robert Mallet said that strain in the earth's crust caused earthquakes.

During the early 1900s, *geologists* (scientists who study the earth) and *seismologists* (earthquake scientists) improved their knowledge of earthquakes. Finally, in the 1960s, a new theory was put forth. Today, the majority of scientists accept this theory as the cause of most earthquakes. It is called the *Plate Tectonic Theory*.

The Plate Tectonic Theory

To understand earthquakes, scientists tell us, we should first know about the structure of our planet. Earth is made of three separate parts. The outer part—called the *crust*—is made of solid rock. The crust is about twenty miles thick beneath the continents. It is about three miles thick beneath the oceans.

Below the crust lies the *mantle*. It is made mainly of hot, solid rock. The mantle extends to a depth of 1,800 miles.

The earth's center is called the *core*. It gets very hot—9,000° F.—inside the core.

In our study of earthquakes, we are most interested in the crust and the mantle. According to the Plate Tectonic Theory, the earth's outer sixty-mile shell is made of a number of separate blocks, called *plates*. The plates extend down through all of the crust and part of the mantle. To get a good idea of the plates, picture the earth as a hard-boiled egg with a cracked shell. The separate pieces of shell are much like the separate plates on our planet.

These plates do not lie still. They move around a bit—perhaps several inches per plate each year. At the places where two plates meet, they bump, grind, and crunch against each other. At these plate borders, the underground rocks are jostled around quite a bit. If enough pressure is placed on the rocks by moving plates, the rocks snap, causing an earthquake. The place where the rocks break is called a *fault*. Moving plates continue to break rock and cause more earthquakes at places where faults have been formed.

Earthquakes aren't the only upheavals that occur at plate boundaries. Sometimes, one plate is pushed beneath another into the hot interior of the earth. When this happens, some rock is melted. The melted rock is called *magma*. Some of the magma rises to the earth's surface, forming volcanoes.

Look at the map of our planet's main earthquake and volcano region. You will see that it forms a pattern. The ring-shaped region surrounding the Pacific Ocean is called the

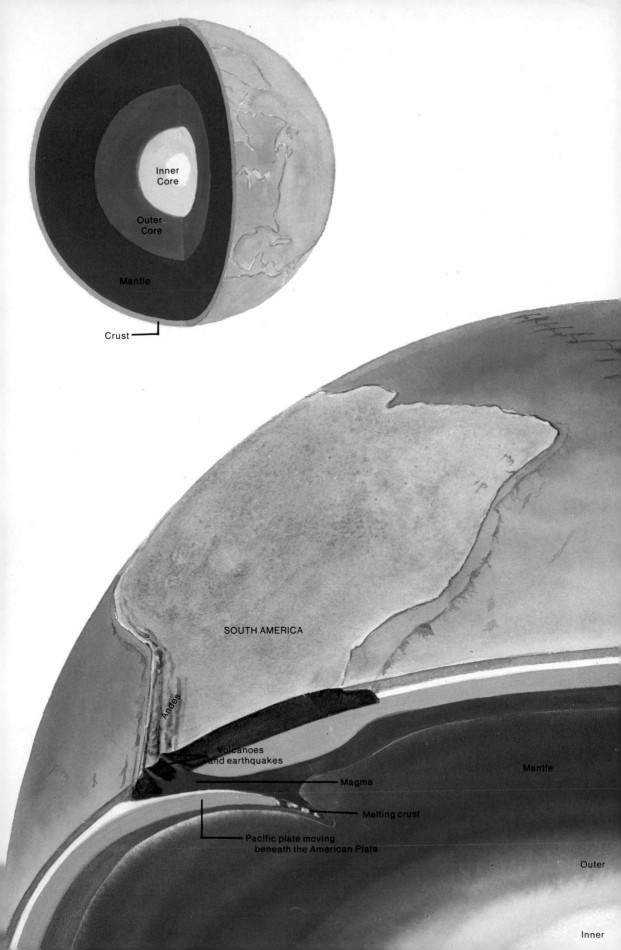

Inner
Core

Outer
Core

Mantle

Crust

SOUTH AMERICA

Andes

Volcanoes
and earthquakes

Magma

Melting crust

Pacific plate moving
beneath the American Plate

Mantle

Outer

Inner

When earth's moving plates bump and grind against one another at their borders, or overlap one another, earthquakes and volcanoes often occur.

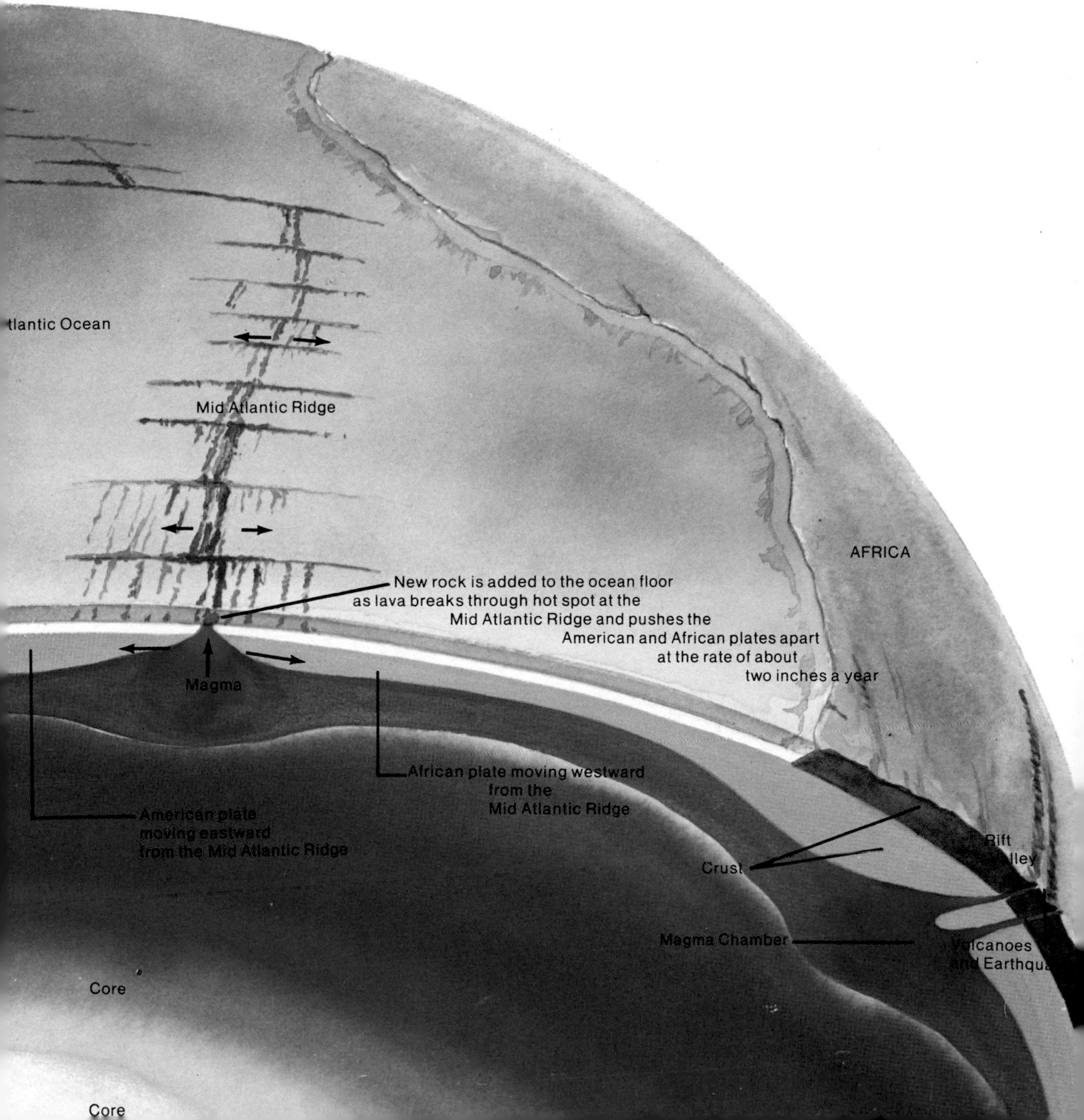

Atlantic Ocean

Mid Atlantic Ridge

New rock is added to the ocean floor as lava breaks through hot spot at the Mid Atlantic Ridge and pushes the American and African plates apart at the rate of about two inches a year

AFRICA

Magma

African plate moving westward from the Mid Atlantic Ridge

American plate moving eastward from the Mid Atlantic Ridge

Crust

Rift Valley

Magma Chamber

Volcanoes and Earthqu

Core

Core

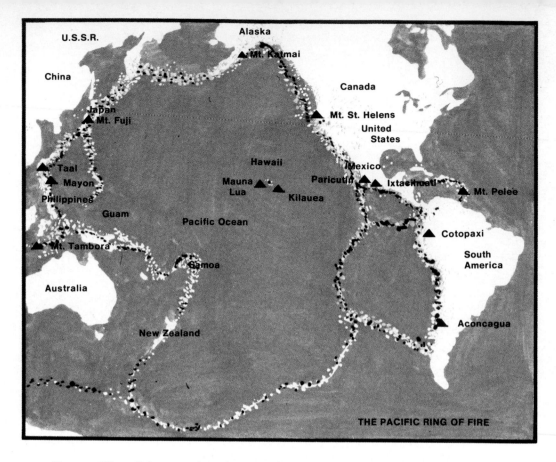

THE PACIFIC RING OF FIRE

Ring of Fire. Many volcanic eruptions and earthquakes have occurred in the Ring of Fire. They are caused by the Pacific Plate and neighboring plates bumping and grinding against other plates. Other major earthquake and volcano regions also occur at places where plates meet.

California's San Andreas Fault

To see how the Plate Tectonic Theory explains earthquakes, let's look at the state of California. It is a major earthquake region in the United States.

Two plates meet beneath California. They are the Pacific Plate and the North American Plate. The 750-mile-long crack between the two plates is called the *San Andreas Fault.*

The Pacific Plate is moving northward at a rate of about two inches per year. As the Pacific Plate creeps northward, it

Shifting land over the San Andreas Fault distorted these cable car tracks on Union Street during the Great San Francisco Earthquake of 1906.

causes rocks to break along the San Andreas Fault. This results in earthquakes. Most of the quakes are small. But in certain places the rocks are locked tightly together. A great deal of pressure is placed on the rocks. Finally, the rocks snap and move in one big thrust. This causes a very large earthquake. This happened in California in 1906. That year, the Great San Francisco Earthquake moved land twenty feet to the north. After a California quake, it is often possible to see how land has moved along the fault. Highways, fences, and even rivers that were once straight are knocked out of line.

There have been many earthquakes along the San Andreas Fault in California. There will surely be more in the future. Later, you will learn how scientists and California residents are preparing for future earthquakes.

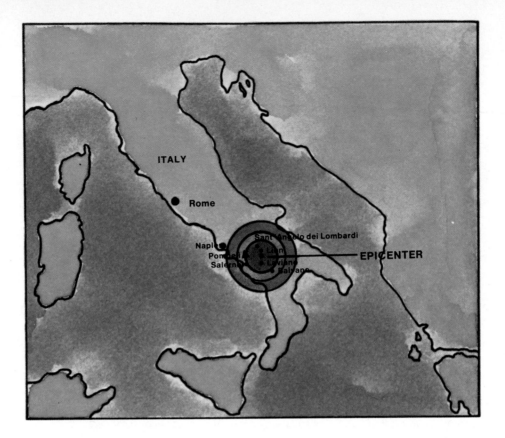

These maps show the epicenters of the 1980 earthquake in southern Italy (above) and the 1964 earthquake in Alaska (below).

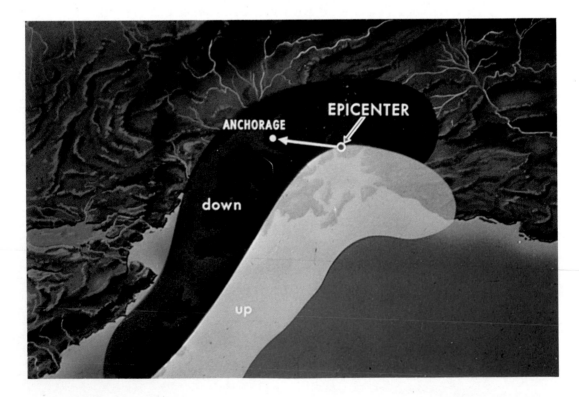

4/HOW EARTHQUAKES KILL AND DESTROY

Scientists use an instrument called a *seismograph* to determine the location and strength of an earthquake. Seismographs record movements in the ground. They can detect very slight movements in the ground at great distances.

The vibrations from an earthquake take time to reach a seismographic station. By timing vibrations at three separate stations, scientists pinpoint the exact location of a quake.

The place beneath the ground where the earthquake begins is called the *focus*. The place on the earth's surface above the focus is called the *epicenter*. The damage is usually the greatest at or near the epicenter. For example, the epicenter of the 1980 Italian quake was near the badly damaged towns of Balvano and Laviano. Earthquakes, however, are not necessarily localized. The ground may break *along* a fault, rather than at just one point.

Scientists also use seismographs to determine the *magnitude,* or strength, of an earthquake. Just as distance is measured in feet or miles, the power of an earthquake is expressed by numbers on the *Richter Scale.* Each whole number on the Richter Scale represents about 30 times as much power as the previous number. An earthquake of magnitude 2.0 is 30 times as powerful as one of magnitude 1.0. One of magnitude 3.0 is 900 times as strong as one of magnitude 1.0.

An earthquake of magnitude 2.0 is very small. In fact, hundreds of such earthquakes occur on our planet every day. Most of them are not even noticed. Earthquakes of magnitude 5.5 or above are the ones that usually do damage. The 1980 earthquake in southern Italy was of magnitude 6.8.

The strongest earthquakes ever recorded were of magnitude 8.9. This happened twice. The first occurred under the Pacific Ocean near Ecuador in 1906. The other occurred beneath the ocean near Japan in 1933. The energy released by each of these 8.9 magnitude quakes was greater than that of a million atomic bombs!

We can't look only at a quake's magnitude to judge its destructiveness. The location of the earthquake also is important. A very strong quake beneath the ocean may do little harm. A lesser earthquake near a big city can kill thousands of people.

Toppling Buildings, Fire, Sea Waves, and Landslides

It is not the shaking of the ground itself that kills. In an open field, even a large earthquake may do little harm to people. People who have survived earthquakes in open areas have compared it to "walking on jelly."

Nor are people usually swallowed up by great cracks in the ground, as you may have seen in movies. Once, during the

Though earthquakes often cause great cracks such as these to appear in the earth, people usually are not swallowed up by them.

This aerial view of Agadir, Morocco shows the almost complete destruction of the town caused by a disastrous 1960 earthquake.

1906 San Francisco earthquake, a cow did get swallowed up by a crack. People knew this had happened only because its tail stuck out of the ground. Such occurrences are very rare, however.

The great killers in earthquakes are toppling buildings, fires, sea waves, and landslides.

You've probably watched a friend build a "house" of blocks. You probably know that there are several ways to destroy such a "house." One way is to hit the blocks and knock them over. Another way is to pound on the table or floor beneath the "house" and let the vibrations knock it down. This second method is the way earthquakes knock down homes and other structures.

An earthquake can flatten a city's buildings. A survivor of the 1960 quake in Agadir, Morocco said that the city looked "as if a giant foot had stepped on it and squashed it flat." When buildings topple and crumble, people inside are killed. People on the streets can be killed by falling walls and debris.

Fire is one of the most devastating results of an earthquake.
The one pictured above, caused by a 1952 earthquake,
raged through a butane refinery in Buena Vista, California.

As the earth shakes, ovens and chimneys are upset. Gas mains break. These events start fires. Fires begun by earthquakes often are deadlier than the falling buildings. This was the case in the San Francisco earthquake of 1906, when fires raged for three days.

Water also can be a big killer. Underwater earthquakes sometimes create huge waves called *tsunamis*. These waves travel toward land at speeds of more than five hundred miles per hour. Out at sea, they are not very tall. But when

*Landslides, another major killer caused by earthquakes, tore
apart an Anchorage elementary school (above) and a downtown
Anchorage street (below) during the 1964 earthquake in Alaska.*

approaching shore, a tsunami can pile up into a wall of water
higher than a five-story building. People near the shore are
drowned, and houses and boats are smashed.

Earthquakes also can shake rocks and earth from
mountains and hills. When rocks and earth begin rolling
downhill, it is called a *landslide.* A 1970 earthquake in Peru
created a giant landslide. Millions of tons of ice, snow, mud,
and rocks were sent tumbling down Mount Huascarán.
Twenty thousand people in the city of Yungay died when they
were buried under the debris.

As you read about some famous quakes in the next
chapter, you will see how toppling buildings, fires, sea waves,
and landslides kill and destroy.

5/SOME MAJOR EARTHQUAKES

Little is known about some of the world's worst earthquakes. Many occurred long before there were newspapers or television crews to describe the devastation. The following earthquakes aren't necessarily the biggest killers or the strongest ever recorded. They are famous because much is known about them.

Lisbon - 1755

In the year 1755, Lisbon, Portugal was a large city of about 250,000 people. It was also an important port city. Many ships went in and out of its harbor.

On November 1, 1755, thousands of people were crowded into Lisbon's churches. It was All Saints' Day—a Christian religious holiday.

At 9:40 A.M., Lisbon was struck by a monstrous quake. During the seven minutes that the ground shook, thousands of buildings collapsed. People were crushed to death in churches and homes. Many who crawled out of the rubble were crushed in the streets by falling buildings. Others were burned to death in the fires that quickly broke out.

Some people went out to the dock, hoping to leave the city by ship. But a second earthquake knocked the dock into the water. Hundreds drowned.

Those near the shore then saw an incredible sight. A tsunami had been created by the shaking of the ground. The huge wall of water smashed the city, drowning thousands more. The wave then rushed out into the Atlantic Ocean. In

A tsunami, caused by the 1755 Lisbon earthquake, smashed into the city (above).

Morocco, 400 miles away, 10,000 people were drowned by a fifty-foot wave. Many hours later, the tsunami struck the island of Martinique—3,500 miles from Lisbon—with a twelve-foot wave.

The Great Lisbon Earthquake killed more than 60,000 people. It also destroyed about two-thirds of Lisbon.

Some good did come out of this terrible disaster. At the time, many people thought that God sent earthquakes to punish people for their sins. But this earthquake had killed innocent babies and children. Surely God couldn't have sent such a punishment. People began to search for scientific explanations.

Five years later, in 1760, English geologist John Mitchell

claimed that earthquakes were caused by the underground movements of rocks. Mitchell hadn't figured out all the details. But scientists were finally on the right track.

New Madrid, Missouri - 1811-1812

In the year 1811 only about seven million people lived in all of the United States. Most of them lived in the eastern part of the country. Fortunately, very few lived in the area near New Madrid, Missouri—a town on the Mississippi River.

On the night of December 15, 1811, the eight hundred people of New Madrid were sleeping in their log cabins. At two o'clock in the morning they were awakened by strange noises. Their cabins were shaking. When the people rushed outside they found that the ground was bucking like a wild horse. Many of the cabins collapsed. A second quake sent more cabins tumbling to the ground.

These quakes were so strong that the course of the Mississippi River was changed temporarily. It actually flowed backward for a time. The quakes also knocked bluffs right into the river.

The New Madrid shocks were felt as far away as Canada, Boston, and New Orleans. In Charleston, South Carolina, the shaking earth caused a church bell to ring by itself. In Kentucky, artist John James Audubon was riding on a horse when the earthquakes struck. He later said that "the ground waved like a field of corn before the breeze."

If New Madrid had been a city of many people and tall buildings, thousands would have died. But the collapse of small log cabins wasn't very dangerous. There were very few deaths or injuries.

Earthquakes—most of them of lesser strength—continued for the rest of 1811 and on into 1812. Jared Brooks of Louisville, Kentucky kept count of the shocks. He noted 1,874 separate quakes. Brooks even built a simple seismograph to help him record the shocks. This was probably the first time that anyone in the United States used instruments to study earthquakes.

Although the New Madrid quakes of 1811-1812 didn't cost many human lives, they did affect the land. Land around New Madrid sank a few feet. The land then filled with water, forming marshes and lakes. One of the lakes—Reelfoot—still exists in western Tennessee.

Reelfoot Lake (below), in western Tennessee, was created by the New Madrid, Missouri earthquakes of 1811-1812.

The fires caused by the 1906 earthquake in San Francisco raged for three days, and left much of the city in ruins (above). During the quake itself, houses toppled (below) and buildings crashed to the ground.

San Francisco - 1906

When the New Madrid earthquakes occurred in 1811-1812, California also had few permanent settlers. But in 1848, gold was found in California. People poured in to search for the yellow metal. San Francisco grew rapidly. It was a city where gold miners bought supplies. By 1906, a half-million people lived in San Francisco. It was a lovely city of homes, theaters, banks, and big hotels.

Even then, California often was struck by small earthquakes. But on the morning of April 18, 1906, San Francisco was rocked by a very strong quake.

At 5:12 A.M., there was a loud roar as the ground began to shake. Cracks opened in the streets. Buildings toppled. Famous singer Enrico Caruso ran out of his hotel yelling, "It's the end of the world!"

The terrible shaking lasted for half a minute. Then a second quake came, even stronger than the first. By the time the shaking ended, much of San Francisco lay in ruins.

Broken gas mains, smashed fireplaces, and overturned stoves started fires. Firemen attached their hoses to hydrants, but there was no water. The water mains had been broken by the quake. The fires, stirred up by the strong San Francisco winds, raged for three days.

About seven hundred people died in the Great San Francisco Earthquake and Fire. About 250,000 homes were wrecked.

Within a short time, the people of San Francisco began to rebuild their city. Today, San Francisco is again one of our prettiest and most interesting cities. But the people who live there know that it could be hit by another earthquake. Today, however, they are better prepared.

Japan-1923

Like California, Japan has been struck many times by earthquakes. For this reason, Japan has been called "The World's Earthquake Factory."

In the early 1900s, famed architect Frank Lloyd Wright was asked to design a large hotel in Tokyo, Japan. Wright knew about Japan's earthquakes. In 1922, he designed the Imperial Hotel with earthquakes in mind. The hotel was built of light materials and the building wasn't sunk very deeply into the soft, marshy ground. Wright hoped the hotel would float like a ship on the sea if the ground started to quake.

Two minutes before noon on September 1, 1923, a huge quake occurred in the area of Japan's Sagami Bay. The nearby cities of Tokyo and Yokohama were hit hard. Many buildings toppled.

Because it was noontime, people had been preparing lunch. Stoves overturned, setting off fires. The fires did the greatest harm. At the Military Clothing Depot in Tokyo, 40,000 people were surrounded by fire. Thirty-eight thousand died from the smoke and flames in that one place. Only those who reached the river survived.

The earthquake caused land beneath Sagami Bay to sink as much as six hundred feet. The changes beneath the bay set off large tsunamis. Thirty-foot waves smashed Japan's coastal cities.

Three killers—falling buildings, fires, and tsunamis—took more than 143,000 lives. In Yokohama, 27,000 people were dead, 40,000 were injured, and most of the buildings were destroyed. In Tokyo, the human toll was even worse. About 100,000 were dead and 40,000 injured.

Tokyo's Imperial Hotel withstood the earthquake—just as

The 1923 earthquake in Japan caused buildings to fall, fires to rage, and tsunamis to crash into coastal cities. This pile of rock and debris in Yokosuka (above) was once a railway station and a high school. Most of the buildings in the city of Tokyo (below) were destroyed.

The 1964 earthquake in Alaska left part of this Anchorage street about twenty feet below the level of the rest of the street.

Frank Lloyd Wright had planned. In fact, hundreds of the homeless later took refuge in the hotel.

The Japanese learned well from this terrible disaster. They designed their new buildings to withstand earthquakes. They widened their streets so people wouldn't be crushed by falling walls. They built new water mains to withstand large shocks. They also created large parks so that people would have open places of refuge during future quakes.

This planning helped. Japan has had many earthquakes in the past sixty years. But none has been as deadly as the 1923 quake.

Alaska - Good Friday, 1964

It was Good Friday—March 27, 1964. At five-thirty that afternoon, many people in Anchorage, Alaska were driving home from work. Others were doing some last-minute Easter shopping in the downtown stores. No one had any idea that much of Alaska's biggest city would soon be destroyed.

At 5:36 P.M. rocks beneath Prince William Sound, 150 miles from Anchorage, suddenly shifted and broke. This caused the strongest earthquake ever recorded in North America. It reached 8.5 on the Richter Scale.

In Anchorage, the shaking earth caused landslides and opened great cracks in the streets and sidewalks. Buildings tumbled to the ground. Houses and stores were smashed and twisted. The sixty-foot-tall control tower at the Anchorage International Airport toppled. A man inside was killed. One movie theater dropped thirty feet when the ground beneath it sank.

Although 75 percent of Anchorage was destroyed or

Huge blocks of earth shifted during the 1964 earthquake in Alaska,
causing great damage, especially in the heavily populated Anchorage
area. Top: A ruined elementary school. Above: One span of a truss
bridge dropped into the Copper River. Below: The section of land in the
foreground sank about ten feet during the earthquake and landslide.

The tracks on this railroad bridge (above) were torn from their ties
and buckled by movement of the river banks during the earthquake. This
wooden fence (below) was buckled and shortened by shifting earth.

damaged, only nine people died there. There was a greater loss of life in other parts of Alaska. Many of the deaths were caused by tsunamis. At the town of Valdez, about thirty people were standing on a dock when a wave suddenly washed them into the sea. At Seward, the earthquake and waves knocked docks and piers into the bay. Oil in storage tanks exploded and soon the oil-coated water was on fire. At Kodiak, ships were carried like bathtub toys into the center of town.

Waves killed people hundreds of miles from Alaska. In Oregon, four children sleeping on a beach were carried out to sea by a wave. In Crescent City, California, a twelve-foot wave smashed the downtown area and killed several people. In Hawaii—2,800 miles from Anchorage—people in the city of Hilo had to run for high ground as waves smashed the shore.

Luckily, this earthquake was centered in an area of small population. The death toll—131—would have been much higher in a more populous area. The property loss—$750 million—also would have been much greater.

After the earthquake, thousands of Alaskans needed medical help, food, and shelter. Telephone systems had been wrecked. Ham radio operators sent messages requesting help for the stricken areas.

The Alaska State Police, the United States Army, the United States Air Force, and the Alaska Air National Guard were some of the groups involved in rescue and recovery operations. Much of the work was done by helicopter and airplane. Food, clothing, and drinking water were flown in. So were doctors, nurses, and medicine. Beds were set up in schools and other buildings. These efforts helped Alaskans survive until they could rebuild their towns and homes.

China - 1976

China has more people than any other country in the world. It also has had some of the worst earthquakes. In 1556, a quake killed about 830,000 people in China. This was the worst earthquake disaster ever. It also ranks as the second-worst natural disaster of any kind. (An 1887 flood in China that killed 900,000 people was the very worst.)

In 1976, China was struck by an earthquake that cost almost as many lives as did the 1556 disaster. The Chinese government released little information about the quake. Much that is known about it was related by non-Chinese people who were there at the time.

At 3:41 on the rainy morning of July 28, 1976, a loud roar awakened millions of people in Hopeh Province. The earth was shaking wildly. The epicenter of the quake was at Tangshan, a coal-mining city of about a million people. One witness said that buildings went down "as if they were made of cards."

Tangshan was almost totally destroyed. Coal tunnels beneath the city collapsed and buildings fell into the tunnels. A hospital fell into one pit. A train fell into another. Miners working the night shift were buried when the tunnels caved in.

In the badly damaged city of Tientsin, a hotel split in half. Throughout the countryside, trees were uprooted by the shaking of the ground. Railroad tracks were twisted like pretzels. Dams fell.

Sixteen hours after the first quake, there was a second that was almost as strong. By this time, however, most survivors were out in fields and streets. There, they were safe from toppling buildings.

The walls of Peking's main department store (above), more than a hundred miles from the epicenter at Tangshan, cracked during the disastrous 1976 earthquake in China.

About 750,000 people died in the China quakes. That's roughly equal to the number of people living in San Francisco today. Hundreds of thousands more were injured.

Think of all the lives that could have been saved if this earthquake had been predicted. On another occasion, Chinese scientists did correctly predict a quake. In the next chapter, we will find out how they did it.

SOME MAJOR EARTHQUAKES

This chart shows dates, places, and death tolls of some well known earthquakes, including those discussed in this chapter:

Date	Place	Deaths
About 1400 B.C.	Crete and nearby islands (where earthquakes, fires, and a volcanic eruption ended the Minoan culture)	Number unknown
856 A.D.	Corinth, Greece	45,000
1268	Asia Minor	60,000
1290	Hopeh Province, China	100,000
1556	Shensi Province, China	830,000 (the largest number ever killed in an earthquake)
1667	Shemaka, Russia	80,000
1669	Mount Etna, Italy	20,000 (by a combined volcanic eruption and earthquake)
1693	Catania, Italy	60,000
1731	Peking, China	100,000
1737	Calcutta, India	300,000
1755	Iran	40,000
1755	Lisbon, Portugal	60,000
1783	Calabria, Italy	50,000
1797	Quito, Ecuador	41,000
1811-1812	New Madrid, Missouri	Number unknown, but thought to be very few
1868	Peru and Ecuador	25,000
1896	Sanriku, Japan	27,000
1906	San Francisco, California	700
1908	Messina, Italy	85,000
1920	Kansu Province, China	180,000

Date	Place	Deaths
1923	Tokyo and Yokohama, Japan	143,000
1935	Quetta, India (now Pakistan)	60,000
1939	Chile	30,000
1939	Erzincan, Turkey	40,000
1964	Alaska	131
1968	Khurasan, Iran	20,000
1970	Peru	67,000
1972	Nicaragua	12,000
1976	Guatemala	23,000
1976	Hopeh Province, China	750,000
1978	Tabas, Iran	25,000
1980	Southern Italy	3,000

Left: The Veterans Administration Hospital in San Fernando, California collapsed during a 1971 earthquake. Right: Two survivors of a 1962 earthquake in Iran that killed 20,000 people sit amid the rubble of their home.

These pictures show earthquake damage that occurred in Managua, Nicaragua in 1972 (top), northeastern Iran in 1970 (above left), Chile in 1960 (above), and Peru in 1970 (left).

6/PREDICTING AND PREPARING

Since records have been kept, earthquakes have killed about 75 million people. With each passing year, an average of 10,000 more die in quakes.

Scientists hope to reduce the yearly death toll in the future by warning people of earthquakes. If people know that a quake is coming, they can go to a safe area. Electricity and gas can be shut off to avoid fires. The water level behind dams can be lowered to prevent floods.

Several small quakes in the United States were correctly predicted during the early 1970s. But—until 1975—some scientists believed it was a waste of time to try to predict a big one.

In early February of 1975, Chinese scientists warned that a major quake was about to strike Liaoning Province. Radio broadcasts advised people to leave their homes. They were told to go out into open fields. Almost everyone listened. On February 4, Liaoning Province was hit by a monstrous quake. In the city of Haicheng, nearly every building was destroyed or damaged. But, because people had left, there were few deaths. Without the warning, a half-million people might have died.

This was the first accurate prediction of a big earthquake. It proved that scientific knowledge of earthquakes can be used to save lives.

Predicting earthquakes is very difficult. Scientists can't look underground where earthquakes begin. Instead, they must work like detectives. They have many instruments to help them study the "clues" that rocks send out before they break.

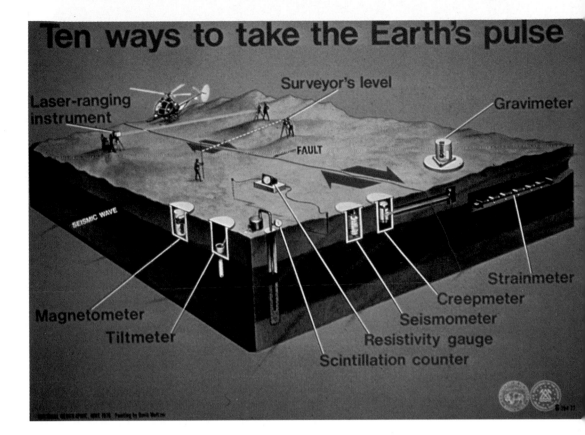

Ten ways to take the Earth's pulse

Laser-ranging instrument · Surveyor's level · Gravimeter · FAULT · SEISMIC WAVE · Magnetometer · Tiltmeter · Scintillation counter · Resistivity gauge · Seismometer · Creepmeter · Strainmeter

The *seismograph* is one of the main instruments scientists use. Often there are small quakes, called *foreshocks,* before a big one hits. If seismographs record a number of foreshocks, these are strong clues that a big quake is coming.

Strainmeters, or *creepmeters,* also are important to earthquake scientists. Strainmeters are placed right across faults. They measure the movement of rocks along a fault. If strainmeters show that the rock is stuck in one place, that means that it may become unstuck in one big earthquake.

Tiltmeters detect very small changes in the tilt, or slope, of the ground. They can detect changes not visible to the human eye. A change in tilt along a fault may mean that rocks are shifting underground. This is another clue that the rocks soon may break.

Scientists also observe well water in earthquake regions. Well water sometimes becomes muddy before a quake. That is because rocks cracking underground add small particles of earth to the water. The level of water in a well sometimes changes before a quake, too. That is because shifting rocks change the pressure on the water. Measuring an element called *radon* in well water also helps scientists predict quakes. The amount of radon often increases before a quake.

There are also electrical, magnetic, and gravitational changes in the ground before a quake. Scientists have instruments to help them measure these changes.

Although it isn't known exactly how they do it, animals often sense when an earthquake is coming. Before quakes, cockroaches twirl in circles, as if confused. Cats run in circles and dogs howl. Birds refuse to land on the ground and frogs jump out of ponds. Rats walk around dizzily. The night before the 1906 San Francisco earthquake, horses kicked wildly in their stalls. In 1964, Kodiak bears in Alaska left their winter sleeping quarters several weeks early. The next day, Alaska was struck by the Good Friday earthquake. In some countries, such as China, farmers report strange animal behavior to earthquake scientists.

Scientists used many of these methods to predict the 1975 quake in China. Before the quake, well water turned muddy. An increase in radon gas was detected. The tilt in the land changed. There were also magnetic and electrical changes in the ground. A wide variety of unusual animal behavior was observed. Most important were the foreshocks felt on February 3. When people feel foreshocks, they are likely to believe that a big quake really is coming.

In 1976, Chinese scientists failed to predict the big quake that cost 750,000 lives. There were no foreshocks or other warning signs. Nor were any warnings detected before the 1980 quake in Italy. This doesn't mean that the clues weren't there. It means only that scientists have much to learn before they can predict earthquakes consistently.

Predicting California Quakes

California has the largest population of any state in the Union—more than 23 million. It also has the San Andreas Fault, where many earthquakes have occurred. A big California quake could be the worst natural disaster in United States history. Falling buildings and fires could kill thousands. Dams could break, causing huge floods.

"California *will* have large earthquakes in the future," says Professor Don Anderson of the California Institute of Technology's Seismological Laboratory. "Almost for sure we will have a big one in the next hundred years. The question is, when exactly will it come?"

Scientists at the United States Geological Survey (USGS) in Menlo Park, California are trying to answer that question. The USGS is the bureau that studies the land. It has many offices throughout the country. At the USGS office in Menlo Park, there is an Office of Earthquake Studies. Its mission is to study and predict California earthquakes.

"We think that we can predict a big quake," says Thomas Burdette, a scientist at the Office of Earthquake Studies. "We expect to see changes in the ground months before a big quake occurs. We have hundreds of instruments set up to help us spot those changes."

The instruments blanket the San Andreas and other California faults. There are seismographs, tiltmeters, and

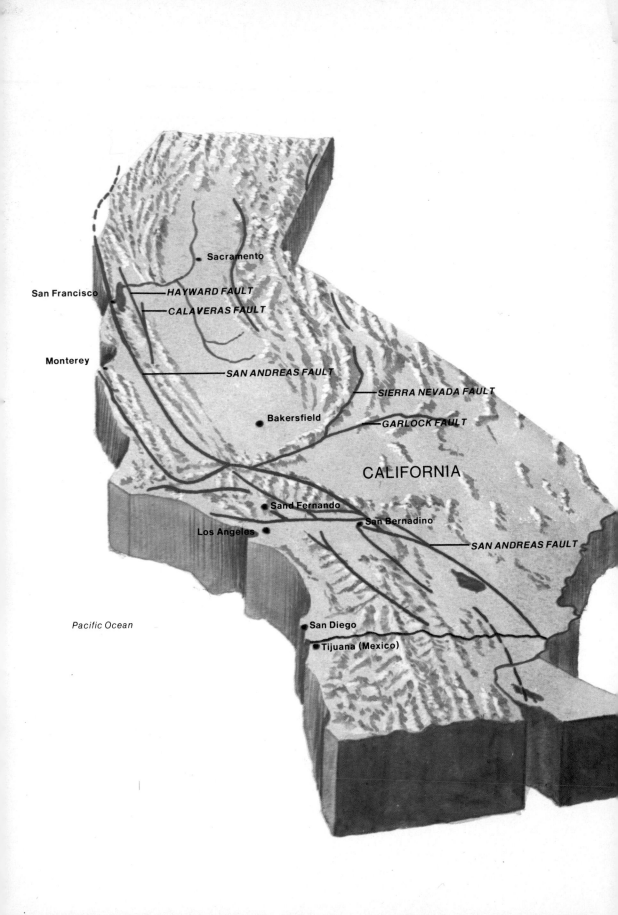

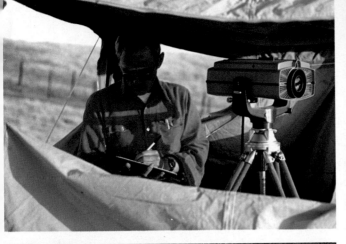

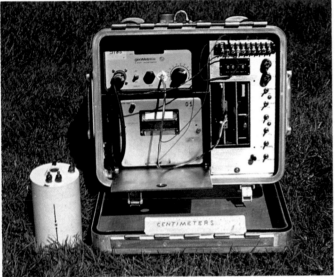

Some of the instruments scientists use to help predict California earthquakes are strainmeters (above left), magnetometers (left), and creepmeters, such as the one above that is installed over the San Andreas Fault.

magnetometers. Strainmeters are set up right across the San Andreas Fault to locate places where rocks may be "stuck."

If USGS scientists see signs of an earthquake, the information will be sent to the governor and local officials. People might be told merely of the chance of an earthquake. Or—if things look serious enough—they might be advised to leave an area.

Preparing for Earthquakes

There is no guarantee that California scientists will detect signs of an earthquake in time to issue a warning. But even without a warning, the death and destruction that occur when the earth shakes can be minimized. All it takes is preparation.

In the event of a big quake, the California Office of Emergency Services would organize rescue efforts. The California National Guard, the United States Army, and the United States Air Force are only three of the groups that could be called on to help. The California National Guard has practiced for earthquakes. It is prepared to fly injured people out of a quake-stricken area. It is prepared to fly in doctors, medicine, and other supplies.

In a big quake, however, it could take many days to bring help to all the injured and homeless. Anita Garcia of the California Office of Emergency Services says that people should be prepared to survive on their own until help arrives.

"In places where earthquakes occur, people should find a place in their homes to store emergency supplies," she says. "They should store food and water. They should have a first-aid kit and know how to use it. Blankets, sleeping bags, flashlights, and portable radios also are important.

"People also should look around their homes to see which areas are dangerous and which are safe. During a quake, stay away from places where heavy objects might fall or where glass might break. Take shelter under a desk or a table for protection."

Californians are preparing for earthquakes in many other ways. Los Angeles and San Francisco schoolchildren are given earthquake drills. They are taught to move under their desks in the event of a quake during school hours. Los Angeles and San Francisco both have held city-wide drills to prepare police, fire fighters, and other personnel for quakes. San Francisco even has an agreement with ferryboat companies. If an earthquake knocks out bridges and roads, people will be carried in and out of the city by boat.

Guarding against Falling Buildings, Tsunamis, Fires, and Landslides

Do you remember the four big killers in earthquakes? In recent years, ways have been found to guard against falling buildings, tsunamis, fires, and landslides.

[Scientists and architects point out that there is no single right way to put up a building in an earthquake region. And there is no way to guarantee that a building will survive a quake.] But some methods of building are better than others. Wood, steel, and reinforced concrete are good building materials. They all can bend a little without breaking. Some places also are better than others for building. ''People shouldn't build on steep slopes or in places where there could be landslides,'' says Thomas Burdette of the Office of Earthquake Studies in Menlo Park. Experts have another good piece of advice: Don't build a house on a fault!

These buildings in Bucharest, Rumania were not built to withstand the devasting 1977 earthquake.

*The tsunami damage along the waterfront in Kodiak
(above) resulted from the 1964 earthquake in Alaska.*

In 1946, an earthquake in Alaska created a tsunami that
drowned a hundred people in Hilo, Hawaii. After that, the
United States set up a system to warn people of approaching
tsunamis. It's called the Pacific Tsunami Warning Center.
With headquarters near Honolulu, Hawaii, this system
consists of more than sixty wave-watching stations in the
Pacific Ocean. The system has saved many lives. A 1960
earthquake in Chile formed tsunamis. Hawaiians were
warned twelve hours before the waves struck. The waves
killed sixty-one people who didn't take the warning seriously.
But those who moved inland survived. The center also warns
people in Russia, Japan, Mexico, Canada, and other countries
of approaching tsunamis.

Fire now is less of a danger than it was in the past.
Fire fighting equipment is better than it was in 1906, when San
Francisco burned. Also, cities now make sure that they have
more than one way to bring in water. In San Francisco and
Los Angeles, the water mains are laid out so that even if some
break, water can be sent in through nearby mains. Both cities
also store water in underground reservoirs. San Francisco
even has big pumping stations that can bring in sea water to
put out fires.

Understanding the land is the main protection against
landslides. By studying the steepness of hills, the wetness of
the soil, and the likelihood of earthquakes in the region,
scientists can tell which areas are prone to landslides. In
California, engineers and county officials work with scientists
to determine whether buildings should go up in certain areas.

The Four Seasons apartment building in Anchorage (below)
crashed to the ground during the 1964 earthquake.

Predicting and Controlling Future Earthquakes

Why do many earthquakes occur during certain years or decades? Can earthquakes be predicted five or even ten years in advance? Do all earthquakes give warning signals?

It may be many years before scientists can answer such questions. Earthquake scientists point out that theirs is a young science.

Some scientists think that one day it may be possible to prevent big earthquakes. During the 1960s, the United States Army was looking for a way to get rid of some poisonous liquids. They pumped them into the ground near Denver, Colorado. Soon there were small earthquakes near Denver. Scientists figured out why. Far beneath the ground the liquids slipped between huge masses of rocks. The liquids "greased" the rocks, making it easier for them to slide into new positions and cause quakes.

USGS scientists then tried an experiment along a small fault in Colorado. They pumped water into the ground. The water greased the rocks and caused small quakes. The scientists found that they could turn earthquakes "on" and "off" whenever they wanted to.

Some scientists think big quakes could be avoided by this method. Liquids could be pumped into the ground, causing a number of small earthquakes. This would be better than the massive movement that brings on a major quake. Scientists aren't ready to try this method in a populated area. If something went wrong, they could wind up *causing* a big quake.

Someday, perhaps, a way will be found to prevent big quakes. In the meantime, scientists will concentrate on predicting, rather than preventing, earthquakes.

Glossary

Aftershock   A minor earthquake that follows a major earthquake as the broken rocks within the earth settle

Core   The very center of the earth

Creepmeter   An instrument that measures the movement of rocks along a fault

Crust   The outside layer of the earth

Earthquake   A shaking of the earth believed to be caused by movement of the earth's plates against or away from one another

Epicenter   The place on the earth's surface directly above the place beneath the ground where an earthquake originates

Fault   A place at the edges of two of the earth's plates where movement of the plates has caused underground rocks to break

Focus   The place beneath the ground where an earthquake originates

Foreshock   A minor earthquake that precedes a major earthquake and originates in the same place as the major earthquake

Geologist   A scientist who studies the earth

Landslide   The rapid slide of earth down a mountain, often caused by volcanic eruption or an earthquake

Magma   Molten rock beneath the surface of the earth

Magnetometer   An instrument that measures magnetic changes in the earth

Magnitude, earthquake   A number on the Richter Scale that indicates the strength of an earthquake

Mantle   The layer of the earth below the crust and above the core

Pacific Ring of Fire   A ring-shaped chain of volcanoes and earthquake regions encircling the Pacific Ocean

Plate Tectonic Theory   A scientific belief that the earth's crust is made up of a number of rigid, slowly moving plates

Radon   A radioactive gas formed by the disintegration of radium that often increases in the earth's crust where an earthquake is about to occur

Richter Scale   An instrument that measures the magnitude of an earthquake

Seismograph   An instrument that detects earthquakes

Seismologist   A scientist who studies earthquakes

Strainmeter   An instrument that measures the movement of rocks along a fault

Tiltmeter   An instrument that measures swelling of the earth

Tsunami   A huge sea wave, sometimes created by an underwater earthquake

Volcano   The opening in the earth's crust through which magma erupts, or the mountain formed by material erupted from the opening

Index

Photo Credits

OFFICE OF EARTHQUAKE STUDIES, UNITED STATES GEOLOGICAL SURVEY (USGS)—
Cover, pages 26 (bottom), 51, 55
USGS—Pages 2, 31, 42, 43, 58, 59
UPI—Pages 4, 6, 7, 8, 10, 11, 28, 29, 30, 39, 40, 46, 48, 49, 57
JUDITH BLOOM FRADIN—Page 14
CAMILLA ALFANO—Pages 15, 18
HISTORICAL PICTURES SERVICE, CHICAGO—Pages 25, 33, 36
DEPARTMENT OF TOURIST DEVELOPMENT, STATE OF TENNESSEE—Page 35
LEN MEENTS (ART)—Pages 19, 22-23, 24, 26 (top), 54

COVER PHOTOGRAPH:—Ground failure and landslide damage in downtown Anchorage resulting
from the 1964 earthquake in Alaska

About the author

Dennis Fradin attended Northwestern University on a partial creative writing scholarship and graduated in 1967. He has published stories and articles in such places as *Ingenue, The Saturday Evening Post, Scholastic, Chicago, Oui,* and *National Humane Review.* His previous books include the Young People's Stories of Our States series for Childrens Press and *Bad Luck Tony* for Prentice-Hall. He is married and the father of three children.

About the artist

Len Meents studied painting and drawing at Southern Illinois University and after graduation in 1969 he moved to Chicago. Mr. Meents works full time as a painter and illustrator. He and his wife and child currently make their home in LaGrange, Illinois.